101 Wacky facts about BUGS & SPIDERS

JEAN WARICHA

SCHOLASTIC INC.
New York Toronto London Auckland Sydney

ISBN 0-590-44892-7
Copyright © 1991 by Parachute Press Inc.
All rights reserved. Published by Scholastic Inc.

Designed by Paula Jo Smith
Illustrated by Bryan Hendrix

12 11 10 9 8 7 6 5 4 3 2   2 3 4 5 6 7/9

Printed in the U. S. A.   01

First Scholastic printing, March 1992

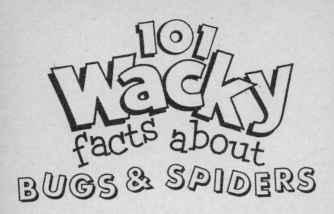

101 Wacky facts about

BUGS & SPIDERS

THE INSECT BOOK OF RECORDS

The goliath beetle of the West Indies is the heaviest bug in the world. The adult beetle weighs 1/4 of a pound. Despite its weight, it can fly. In fact, the goliath beetle can fly like a bullet and can crash through plate glass windows!

Fleas can jump eight inches into the air. This is about 100 times their height. If a human could do this, he or she would be able to jump over a 40-story building!

Moths have been around for over 140 million years. Just think—they were flying around while the dinosaurs lived!

The fairy fly or tiny wasp is so, so tiny that two of these flies can fit comfortably on the period at the end of this sentence.

Who bit me? The "no see me" is a tiny biting fly. It is 1/16 of an inch long—about the same thickness as a paper match.

There are more types of beetles than any other kind of insect. If you started to write down their names at a rate of one name each minute, it would take you five months to finish the list!

The hummingbird is known to beat its wings about 80 beats a second. But a housefly can beat its wings more than 10,000 beats a minute—when it's in a hurry, that is.

Flies are speed demons. How speedy are they? During short flights, the fly can travel up to 50 miles per hour!

"Centipede" means 100 feet. But some centipedes have only 15 pairs of legs, while others have as many as 170!

Wasps may have been the world's first papermakers! The paper wasp builds a nest out of the wood it chews up. The nests hang inside barns and sheltered areas.

Jiminy cricket! When one scientist timed a snowy tree cricket, he found that this incredible insect chirped 90 times a minute—5,400 times an hour!

Termites are among the longest living of all insects. Records show one happily married couple of termites lived together for 25 years!

How quaint! Butterflies weigh as much as two rose petals. But these dainty creatures fly thousands of miles each year.

It would take 100,000 average-sized ants to weigh as much as one man.

Grasshopper steak! Grasshoppers are so nutritious that pound for pound, they are three times as nutritious as red meat!

Whirligig beetles are bugs that live in pools, ponds, or streams. What's so special about them? Well, they have strange eyes, that's what! One half of each eye looks up and the other half looks down.

LET'S EAT!

It is the female mosquito that wants your blood! The male mosquito is quite harmless. Your blood is needed to boost the female's egg production. It is also the female mosquito that buzzes, so beware!

Crickets are vegetarian by choice—but if caged without food, crickets will devour each other!

Insects never seem to get enough food. In a single day some young insects eat more than twice their weight. If you weighed 100 pounds, you would need to eat 20 loaves of bread, 4 pounds of butter, 12 dozen eggs, 2 hams, and drink 15 gallons of milk in order to consume twice your weight. Hungry anyone?

The praying mantis likes to eat slowly, enjoying every bite. It eats its insect victims by selecting the tasty parts and discarding the rest!

Termites eat cellulose—a chemical contained in plants, seeds, wood, rags, and even paper. Cellulose is so important to termites that in some termite nests, they have "gardens" for growing their own cellulose-based foods!

THE ANT

Ants can carry 50 times their own weight. That is like a person lifting a small elephant!

Cleanliness is important to ants. They wash themselves from 15 to 20 times a day. In fact, when an ant wakes up, it stretches and cleans every part of its body before starting its busy day!

Harvester ants are very busy ants. They build anthills with as many as 400 rooms!

Ants find the way back to their nests by leaving chemical trails. How do they do it? The ant runs a short way, stops, presses its body to the ground, and leaves a spot of chemical. An ant is sure to find its way home!

Woof, woof! The bulldog ants of Australia are among the largest of all ants. They measure 1 1/2 inches long. They can run very fast and leap several inches. Bulldog ants actually chase humans who come near their nests.

Biting ants have been used in Brazil to close humans' wounds. After the ants clamp their jaws on the broken skin, the doctor snips off their bodies, leaving their jaws holding the skin together, making an ant stitch!

Talk about bad table manners! Ants eat anything as long as it is juicy. When an ant takes solid food into its mouth, it squeezes the juice out and spits out the rest!

Aphids, or plant lice, produce a sweet "honeydew" from the sap of plants. Groups of ants watch over whole herds of aphids and then "milk" them by stroking their sides until a sweet liquid oozes out. Ants love this honeydew so much that they take great care of their "cows."

Are they lazy or what? Since the Japanese samurai ants cannot take care of themselves, they get slave ants to feed them, take care of their young, and keep their nests neat and clean.

Names can be misleading! Carpenter ants don't eat wood, but they live in damp wooden floorboards and trees. Fire ants don't like the heat, but get their name from their reddish-black color and painful bite.

Now that's what I call a buddy! Since ants have two stomachs, they can be generous. So, when a full ant meets a hungry ant, it can pass some of its food to the mouth of the hungry ant.

The driver ant of Africa will drive you away, that's for sure! This voracious ant eats every kind of insect, bird, or small animal. It will even eat large animals or humans who do not get out of its way. Even elephants get out of the driver ant's way!

What a way to live! Drawer ants of Africa only march on gray days or at night. Sunshine kills them.

Honey ants are fed to the bursting point by their fellow ants. They grow to look like honey-colored pearls. These poor ants are so full they cannot even walk, and sometimes they even explode!

BUGS AND HUMANS

The scarab beetle was sacred in ancient Egypt. It is sometimes called the dung beetle, because it rolls animal dung into a ball to feed its young. The ancient Egyptians associated this beetle with their sun god, Ra, who rolled the sun across the sky!

Cucuyo beetles of South America have dots on their bodies that glow in the dark! They can produce enough light for people to read by. In fact, during the construction of the Panama Canal, a surgical operation was conducted at night by the light from a jar full of cucuyo beetles!

In the 14th and 16th centuries, the rat flea was responsible for the deaths of millions of people in Europe and Asia. The fleas carried a germ that caused a disease known as the Black Death.

For centuries cricket fighting was a sport in China. Records of famous crickets were kept by the Chinese, just like the records we keep of famous racehorses! Before a cricket fight, crickets were fed a special diet of rice, boiled chestnuts, and mosquitoes!

The silkworm is not a worm at all. It is a caterpillar. When only a few weeks old, the worm stops eating and a very thin silk thread comes from its mouth. It winds this thread around its body to make a cocoon. If left alone, it will turn into a moth. But some silkworms are raised on farms, and people collect and use their silk. It takes the thread of about 20,000 cocoons to make a pound of silk. According to Chinese legends, this silk fiber was first used in 2700 B.C.

One species of crickets is widely eaten in Thailand. The crickets are fried and sold in baskets by the locals. People say that they taste like lettuce.

No more Chinese food for me, thanks! Giant water bugs are quite tasty. They live underwater and catch small frogs or snails for food. They are so tasty that they are imported to California to give a particularly "unusual" flavor to some Chinese food!

Pass the insects, please! Insects have a high salt content in their blood. In some countries they are used to spice up food!

Termites can be eaten! In Africa, termites are eaten raw—the natural way. But you can also enjoy termites fried and salted. In fact, you can find salted termites in plastic bags sold in many places all over the world. Check with your local supermarket!

Crunch! The American Indians loved fried-up caterpillars. They saved them for a special treat.

Hide beetles have an unusual job. They are kept in special enclosures in natural history museums. They clean the meat from bird, animal, and fish skeletons down to the bare bone, leaving the bones spic and span.

South African beetles are so poisonous that natives of the Kalahari desert put them on the tips of their hunting arrows.

The silverfish is not a fish at all!
It is a soft-bodied insect that loves to
feed on wallpaper, bookbindings,
and clothing!

Red pigment is obtained from
dried, ground-up bodies of scale
insects. It takes 70,000 insects to
make a pound of red dye.

Honey ants were often munched on by the Mexican Indians. These syrup-filled ants were enjoyed as a kind of candy.

In both China and Japan, cicadas and crickets are kept as musical pets. They are placed in small cages just like birds. Every wealthy family has a chorus of crickets to listen to!

ATTACK!

The killer bees are coming! Killer bees are originally from Africa and not from the American continent. But in 1957, a scientist imported "killer bees" to Brazil for an experiment. Unfortunately, during the experiment, 26 killer bees escaped by accident. By 1988, there were over one trillion killer bees in South America, Central America, and Mexico. Next stop, the United States!

The praying mantis holds up its front legs so it looks like it's praying. In fact, it is really waiting to kill!

Termite soldiers defend the termite queen! Although termites are deaf and blind, they have powerful jaws and pincers. Their heads look like spray guns. When an enemy attacks the nest, termite soldiers spray poison and are rid of the enemy in a splash!

The bombardier beetle has been using the gas-attack technique for centuries to ward off its enemies. When attacked, this beetle ejects a drop of fluid that turns into a jet of smokelike gas when it hits the air. The beetle can fire four or five rounds before its supply is used up!

Insects have to be careful of plants! Several kinds of plants eat insects. The Venus flytrap is a famous one. It has a hinged pair of leaves that produces nectar. When a fly lands on the leaf, it snaps shut and eats the sweetened fly.

If it's hungry, stay away! The praying mantis is fearless and will attack any living prey it can. The praying mantis is a cannibal from birth, and it even eats its own kind!

One bee sting can be deadly. However, once a person was stung 2,243 times and survived!

African killer bees attack with great fury, in large numbers, and sting many times. A few hundred stings will kill anyone! Killer bees have killed large numbers of pigs, cows, and other animals. It is believed that several hundred people have also been victims of the African killer bee.

Assassin bugs hunt and kill their enemies. One kind of assassin bug is called the kissing bug because it often bites people on the face and injects its poison.

Some ground beetles can run very fast to get away from their enemies. But click beetles drop to the ground and play dead!

Strong chemicals used in insecticides on plants destroy bees—and we need bees to pollinate crops so they will grow. However, the killer bee is the only bee that can survive being sprayed by insecticide. So beware! Killer bees are on their way!

There is a certain breed of South American bee that can kill up to 150 people—each time with a single sting!

A honeybee only uses its stinger in self-defense because it dies soon after using it. A bumblebee, however, can use its stinger many times.

A flea is difficult to kill. It has no neck, no waist, and no wings. And its body is covered with armored plates! Good luck!

Keep on the lookout! If you ever see an insect that is red, yellow, and black, stay away! Insects with these colors are often poisonous!

The female horsefly feeds on blood. A bite from her bleeds longer than other insect bites because her saliva contains a chemical that prevents blood from clotting.

Sleep tight. Don't let the bedbugs bite! You hope! The bedbug belongs to a small group of bloodsucking bugs.

Among the insects that never fly are fleas, lice, and bedbugs, which all live by sucking animal or human blood for nourishment.

Have you ever heard a moth hiss? Well, the Death's Head Moth actually hisses through its nose when threatened!

FROM ONE BUG TO ANOTHER

Just a little song and dance!
Bees do a little dance to call to the
other bees when they find nectar.
It's probably because they are so
happy to find a good supply!

Wood beetles knock their heads
against wood if something disturbs
them. There are people who do this
too!

Insects can send messages over amazingly long distances. The female moth, for example, produces a scent that a male moth can smell a mile away.

What a life! The cicada is more often heard than seen. Who doesn't recognize its hum on a warm summer night? It actually takes a cicada 17 years to grow from an egg to an adult. But the adult cicada lives only from four to six weeks. And the adult cicada doesn't eat!

Who's the boss? When the king and queen termite first live together, they are about the same size. But as the years go by, the queen gets larger and larger—sometimes 500 times her original size! The king stays tiny!

The backswimmer bug looks like a boat moving in the water. It swims on its back, propelling itself along with its long, hairy hind legs. In the winter, when a pond freezes over, you can see backswimmer bugs walking around upside down under the ice!

ITSY BITSY SPIDER

Most people think that spiders are insects! This is false. Spiders are classified as arachnids (uh-RACK-nids). Unlike insects, spiders have neither wings nor antennae, and they have eight legs instead of six.

Most spiders cannot see very well. They sit on their webs with their legs touching a single strand. The movement of the web tells them when an insect has landed on the silky strands. Ring the dinner bell!

A liquid diet! Spiders cannot chew or swallow their food. They consume only liquids. They turn their insect prey into a kind of soup and suck it all up!

If you're a male spider, you'd better dance well! When a male and female spider are ready to mate, the male spider does a special dance. Sometimes the female dances, but other times she just ignores the male's dance and eats him up!

If a spider gets into a fight and loses a leg, a new leg will soon grow back in its place.

Spiders don't taste with their mouths like humans do. Instead they taste with their feet!

Male tarantulas live for about 10 years. Females can live as long as 25 years! How can you tell them apart? Until these spiders are fully grown, it is impossible!

Spiders mummify their victims! They kill their prey and then wrap them in a liquid silk that dries on the victims upon contact. The mummylike victims can be eaten right away or saved for later.

I'm out of here! The deadly black widow spider has a bite 15 times more potent than the bite of a rattlesnake!

Funnel web spiders spin a funnel-shaped web of sticky spider silk at the entrance of their homes. Insects that try to pass this funnel get stuck in the silk, and the spiders jump out and eat them. Funnel web spiders are the deadliest spiders in the world. Their venom spreads pain through the victim's body and makes it impossible to breathe, killing the victim very quickly. Scientists have recently developed an antitoxin to their venom, which can save the victim's life if administered immediately. Luckily, there are no funnel web spiders in the United States. They live only in Australia.

Who wants a hamster when you can have a tarantula? Tarantulas are actually not dangerous to humans. If you handle them roughly, these spiders may give you a painful bite. But they are safe enough to keep as pets!

The poisonous black widow spider has a red hourglass marking on her body and can be found in every state in the United States except Hawaii and Alaska.

SURPRISE, SURPRISE, SURPRISE

Insects sleep with their eyes open. They don't have eyelids, so they have no way to close them.

Only adult male crickets chirp! The females, who have ears on their knees, just listen. Young wingless children crickets make no noise at all. Does this sound like your family?

Insects are related to crabs and lobsters! Like these sea animals, their skeletons are on the outside of their bodies.

Bees have little brushes and baskets on their legs for collecting and storing pollen.

In the West Indies some people use fireflies in their huts when they run out of candles!

Contrary to popular belief, flies don't get bigger as they age. Small houseflies do not become big houseflies. Flies are actually born full grown. Bees are also born full grown.

Praying mantises make good pets. They even like to have their backs stroked, and will eat from a person's hand!

Bugs have no lungs! An insect breathes through many tiny openings, or pores, on its abdomen. Each of these pores is an entrance to a tube called a trachea, which takes in air like a person's windpipe. An insect can have hundreds of these tiny tubes inside its abdomen. Imagine how you would look if you breathed through your stomach!

An ordinary housefly is a good acrobat. It can walk upside-down on ceilings and can land on almost any surface.

So you thought that a firefly was a fly? Wrong! Fireflies, or lightning bugs, are neither flies nor bugs. They are classified as beetles.

The royal life is a long life! All bees die in winter, except for the queen, who hibernates.

A female termite queen may live for as long as 15 years, and for much of her life she will lay one egg every three seconds!

Insect specialists have found that chirping crickets can tell you the temperature! Just count the chirps emitted in 15 seconds. Add 40 to that number and this will tell you the degrees in Fahrenheit with surprising accuracy!

So what are you waiting for?